1 MONTH OF
FREE
READING

at

www.ForgottenBooks.com

By purchasing this book you are eligible for one month membership to ForgottenBooks.com, giving you unlimited access to our entire collection of over 1,000,000 titles via our web site and mobile apps.

To claim your free month visit:

www.forgottenbooks.com/free1192801

ISBN 978-0-331-47947-8
PIBN 11192801

MINUTES

OF THE

Fifty-ninth Annual Assembly

OF THE

DISCIPLES of CHRIST

OF THE

Goldsboro and Raleigh District

In Eastern N. C. and Va.

CONVENED WITH

ST. PETER CHURCH OF CHRIST. SMITHFIELD, N. C.

Oct. 20, 21, 22 & 23, 1931·

Eld. B. C. Whitfield, Compiler.***
Eld. I. W. Faison, Secretary, Route 2. Box 5, Faison, N. C.

The next Annual Assembly will be held with the King Chapel
Church of Christ, Kinston, N. C. Oct. 17-20, 1932.

THE WHITFIELD PRESS, NORFOLK, VA.

The Late Elder B. C. Whitfield,

PROCEEDINGS

Smithfield, N. C., Oct. 20, 1931.

According to the decision of the General Assembly at Goldsboro, the 59th. Annual Assembly met on the above mentioned date with the St. Peter Church of Christ, Eld. W. A. Fordham pastor. The devotionals were conducted by the Presiding Officers. Eld. Lofton lined hymn no.45, "A charge to keep I have," and Chief Davis read the 18th. chapter of Matthew. Eld. J. S. Johnson offered a very fervent prayer. The Asst. Chief then sang hymn no. 195 and we all joined in a hand of fellowship. After a few preliminary remarks the Chief appointed Eld. J. D. Henry to preach the Introductory Sermon. Eld. J. H. Frazier lined hymn no. 129, "Am I a soldier of the cross?" and introduced Eld. Henry who chose a text from Ezekiel 1:20 "And the Lord showed me four carpenters." Subj: Christian carpentry." He handled his subject in a masterly manner and punctuated his sermon with frequent allusions to poetry and scripture. His sermon was appropriate and interesting. Eld. Frazier extended the gospel invitation. The finance solicitors took an offering of $2.00. The Assembly adjourned until 2: 30. Benediction by the Chief. At the appointed hour Eld. Frazier lined hymn no. 156 and prayer was offered by Eld. J. H. Harper, the Chief then sang "My soul by on thy guard," and pronounced the house in order for the dispatch of business. The Chief then delivered his Annual Address. He first thanked the delegation for the honor, esteem and confidence placed in him, and expressed his wholehearted desire for the connection's progress, and how he would remain loyal to the Assembly regardless to his official standing. The Asst. Chief. Eld. Lofton made quite a timely speech. After thanking the delegation, he urged upon them the duty of unity and co-operation in the progress of the church. He laid great emphasis upon the words of the apostle: "Be not decieved, God is not mocked, whatsoever a man sow that shall he also reap. Gal. 6:7. The Supervisor, Elder C. R. D. Whitfield made his Annual Address which will be found on another page. The Secretaries made brief talks, thanking the delegation for the honor, esteem and confidence placed in them. During the recess hour the Council Board was called in extra session to investigate a matter between one of the assembly officers and another brother which was settled in love and union. Eld. W. R. Steeley, Chief of the Washington-Norfolk District, accompanied by Eld. T. B. Hoyel and Eld. W. G. Vincent were introduced and made welcome, also Eld Walder of the southern assembly. After remarks by Past Chief, W. A. Fordham, a committee on nomination was appointed as follows: Elds. G. R. Fields, J. E. Dunn, J. S. Johnson, J. L. Lee and J H Smith. This committee recieved its charge and retired for deliberation. The visiting Elders then brought greetings from the Southern and Eastern assemblies

Report of Committee on Permanent Organization

COMMITTEE REPORT.

Brother Chief and brothers, We your Committee on Permanent Organization wish to make the following report: We Nominate for Chief, Elder H. D. Davis; Asst., Elder S. L. Lofton; for Secretary, Elder B. C. Whitfield; for Asst. Elder I. W. Faison.

Elders G. R. Fields,
J. E. Dunn,
J. S. Johnson,
J. L Lee and
J. H. Smith,
COMMITTEE.

It was proposed by Eld. W. A. Fordham and agreed that the Report be recieved. adopted. It was proposed and agreed that the order of business be as heretofore, adopted. The Chief and house began to appoint the various committees:

1. ON DIVINE WORSHIP, Bro. John Dunn, Sisters Janie Brewington Flossie Saunders, Cora Dunn and Estelle Rowe.
2. ON STATISTICS, Elders W. G. Best and L. D. Wiggs.
3. ON SUNDAY SCHOOLS, Bros. Frank Adams, Louis B. Britt and Sisters Anna Stolon, Roberta Penny, W. G. Best, Lucille Burnett and Luana Williams.
4. ON ORDINATION, Elds. J. C. Artice, J. D. Henry and C.H.Cordon.
5. ON FINANCE, Elds. W. A. Fordham and A Parker.
6. MARSHALS, Elds. J H. Smith and G. R. Fields.
7. MAIL CARRIER, Eld. A. B. Aycock.
8. FINANCE SOLICITORS, Elds. W. B. Parks, J.H. Rouse, A.B.Aycock.
9. ON MINISTERIAL CHARACTER, Elds. J. Raynor, W. M King, O. S. Lucas, J. Wilks, J. R. Best and H. L. Shepherd
10. ON TEMPERANCE, Elds. G. B. Borden, C. D. Royal, J. H. Frazier, J. E. Dunn and Sister Fannie Pettiford.
11. ON GRIEVANCES, Elds. P. H. Howell, R. B. Banks, J. Graham, Z. V. Quinerly and K. K. Wiley.
12. ON EULOGY, Elds. R. Croom, A. L. Hart, G. E. Ellis, W. I. Hawkins, J L. Lee and Bro. J. L. Dunn.
13. ON NEW CHURCHES, Elds. J. T. Foy, J. S. Johnson, W. M. Mc Arthur. Bros. Nat Aulston and W. A. Moseley.
Elder D. B. Bynum came foward and made a talk concerning his leave of absence for some time from the connection and his work with the Method-ist brethren. It was proposed and agreed that Elder Bynum be reinstated and by the payment of $5.00 his name be placed on the Elders roll.

Report of Committee on Preaching

Brother Chief and brethren: We recoommend that Elder T. B. Hoyel preach tonight and Elder A B. Aycock alternate; at 11:00 o'clock tomorrow, Eld. W. G. Vincient to preach and Elder A. Parker alternate, adopted.
Elder P. R. Mewborn made remarks concerning his trip to New York and how he found the work. Elder B. J. Gregory made a few timely remarks stating that this will be the last assembly he will meet.
Benediction by the Chief.

Tuesday Night Session

After voluntary song and prayer offerings the choir sang a number of beautiful selections and the Secretary introduced Mrs. Flossie Saunders, the Mistress of Ceremonies who took charge of the program and rendered an excellent program. Elder J. H. Rouse read from the 18th. chapter of St. Luke. Prayer was offered by Eld. G E. Ellis. The choir sang another selection. Mrs. D. A. Stevens was introduced and delivered a splendid Address of welcome on behalf of the local church. Rev. Dr. Smith (white) the pastor of the Presbyterian Church, was introduced and delivered a splendid Address on behalf of the white churches. His address was ably responded to by Elder B. C. Whitfield. Rev. J. H. Todd was introduced and delivered a splended address on behalf of the Negro churches of the city. His address was responded to by Eld. J. D. Henry. Prof. J. T. Gregg was introduced and delivered a splendid address on behalf of the schools and Negro busi-ness. Eld. W. G Vincient responded. Miss Roberta Whitley and Mrs. Flos-ie Saunders sang a beautiful duett. Eld T. B. Hoyel being sick, Elder A.B. Aycock made a few timely remarks and the finance solicitors took an of-fering which amount was $4.05, after which the pastor and Secretary made the announcements and the choir sang doxology. Benediction by Eld. Lofton.

Wednesday Morning Business Session

The Assembly met pursuant to adjournment at 9:30 with the Chief Eld. Davis in the chair. Eld. C. R. D. Whitfield lined hymn 115, "Blest be the tie that binds." The Chief read the 6th. chapter of Galations and commented on the lesson. A very fervent prayer was offered by Eld. A. Parker. The Supervisor lined hymn no. 149, "Come Holy Spirit heavenly Dove." The Chief, after a brief lecture pronounced the house in order for the dispatch of business. The Supervisor produced the mortgage and notes that had been held for a number of years by the Bank of Wayne against school property. They had been paid off by the Trustees of the Assembly.

It was proposed by Eld. Aycock that the minute of the previous day session be read Eld. B. C. Whitfield and Chief W. R. Steeley made talks concerning The Christian Reformer, a new paper edited by Mr. C. L. Whitfield at 2311 Hanson Ave., Norfolk, Va This paper is an official organ for brotherhood of Disciples of Christ published monthly at 60 cents per year.

The order of business was calling the roll of Elders. (see Elders roll) Adjournment for preaching. Benediction.

Wednesday Morning Preaching Service

Elder C. R. D. Whitfield lined hymn no. 126, "Alas! and did my Savior bleed." Elder A. Parker read St. Luke chapter 4. Eld. C. H. Cordon offered a fervent prayer and Eld. Parker lined hymn 217, "Try me oh Lord and search the ground." He then introduced Elder. W. G. Vincient of the W. N. District, who chose for a text: "Are not Abana and Pharpar, rivers of Damascus better than all the waters of Israel?" 2 Kings 5:12. Eld. Vincient did justice to the subject and a soul stirring service prevailed. Elder Parker extended an invitation. The finance solicitors, took an offering to the amount of $3.06. Benediction by the Asst. Chief Eld. Lofton.

Wednesday Afternoon Business Session

The Chief called the house to order, singing "My soul be on thy guard," and the Secretary continued to call the roll of Delegates and churches. (see statistical table and delegate roll)

REPORT OF COMMITTEE ON DIVINE WORSHIP

Brother Chief and brethren: We recommend to preach tonight, Elder T. B. Hoyel alternated by Eld. J. S. Johnson, and for tomorrow morning, Eld. W. R. Steeley alternated by Eld. W. G. Best. Benediction by the Chief.

Wednesday Night Preaching Service

After voluntary song service the Star Banner sang two beautiful selections. The choir sang no. 227 and the 11th. chapter of Exodus was read by Elder J. S. Johnson Prayer was offered by Eld. A. L. Hart, after another selection by the choir, the finance solicitors took an offering to the amount of $6.25. Eld. Johnson introduced Eld. T. B. Hoyel, who sang one of his favorite spirituals, "Let the train run easy," and took a text from the 11 chapter of Exodus and 7th. verse, text: "Not a dog shall move his tongue." The speaker preached a soul stirring sermon. Elder Johnson exposited on the discourse. Announcements by the Secretary and Pastor, doxology by the choir. Benediction by the Chief.

Thursday Morning Session

The Assembly met pursuant to adjournment, Chief Eld. Davis in the chair. After the devotional period the Chief pronounced the house in order for business It was proposed and agreed that we hear the minute of the previous days session. Eld. J. C. Artice made a brief and very encouraging talk to the churches and pastors to do all that they can to raise the budget, his church having gone over the top with $52.70. A vote of thanks was extended him and his church. The Secretary re called the roll. Adjournment for preaching. Benediction.

Thursday Morning Preaching Service

According to the appointment, at 11:00 o'clock the Memorial Service for Elds. H. A. Whitfield, F. Graham and A. Berry was conducted by Elders W. R. Steeley and W. G. Best. Eld. J. H. Smith lined hymn no. 245 "Asleep in Jesus," and read Job, chapter 14 and prayer was offered by Eld. G. R. Fields. The congregation joined in singing "O God our help in ages past." The Secretary Eld. I. W. Faison read the obituaries and Eld. W. G. Best introduced Elder W. R. Steeley who chose his text from Psalms 37:23. "The steps of a good man are ordered by the Lord" He handled the subject in a masterly manner and preached a great sermon to the satisfaction of all present. Elder W. G. Best exposited in an intelligent way and closed with a word of prayer. The finance solititors raised $3.82. Benediction.

Thursday Afternoon Session

The Chief called the house to order and began to recieve the reports of the various committees.

REPORT OF MINISTERS' and LAYMEN'S CONFERENCE

Brother Chief and Brethren, We wish to report that we held a splendid session this year at St. Luke Church, Goldsboro, which was well attended, and the same officers were re-elected and Prof. J. F. Whitfield was appointed critic. Many interesting topics were discussed.

Elder. W. G. Best, President,
Elder J. C. Artice, Vice President,
Bro. D. P. Holloway, Secretary.

ON MINISTERIAL CHARACTER

Brother Chief and Brethren: We wish to make our report as follows: We find all ministers in gospel order until now.

Eld. W. M. King.	Eld. J. R. Best,
Eld. O. L. Lucas,	Eld. James Wilks,
Eld. J. F. McLaurin,	Eld. H. L. Sepherd,
Eld. J. Raynor,	committee.

ON GRIEVANCES

Brother Chief and Brethren, We wish to submit our report: We disposed of all of the cases that came before us except the church at Running Branch.

Elders K. K. Wiley,	P. H. Howell,	R. B Banks,
Z. V. Quinerly,	James Graham,	committee.

ON EULOGY

Brother Chief, Our report is as follows: There have been reported 60 deaths including six Elders and one Deacon.

Elders R. Croom,	J. L. Lee,	A. Hart,
G. E. Ellis,	W. J. Hawkins,	J. L. Dunn, committee.

ON BIBLE SCHOOLS

Brother Chief, We wish to make the following report and recommendations: In the no. 2 district we have 39 old schools, one new school and nine representing; we recommend that all teachers and superintendents be financial members of some church, and that theyremain in preaching services and co-operate with the pastor, and that the pastor attend the Bible School each Sunday wherever he may be, and that all pastors avoid as much as possible regular meetings during the Convention, and that Deacons attend.

Brothers Frank Adams,	Louis Britt,	Sisters M. G. Best,
Lula Burnett,	Ann Williams,	Roberta Penny, Anna Streeter, comm.

ON TEMPERANCE

Brethren, Our report is as follows: Our brothers are living temperate as a whole, and we admonish those who are not to do so as "we are the light of the world." Respectfully submitted,

Elds. G. B. Borden,   J. H. Frazier,
C. D. Royal,   J. E. Dunn,
F. Pettiford,   committee.

REPORT OF SUPERVISOR

Smithfield, N. C., Oct. 19, 1931.

Chief and Brothers of the G. R. D., I beg leave to submit my Annual Report: First of all, we thank Almighty God for his loving kindness and blessing that He has bestowed upon us from last October until this. Since the last Assembly four of our Elders have fallen asleep in death Elds. J. S. Ray, Alex Berry and H. A. Whitfield. We loved them, but God loved them best and we know not who will be the next, so let us live right so that we can die right with God and Christ. The Brotherhood and Churches in our District are in a fairly good condition, just a few need to be lined up. We have good news to tell the brotherhood about our school. (1) We borrowed money enough from the Brotherhood and churches to take up the mortgage and note from the Building and Loan Association of Goldsboro. (2) Because they said they could not run us over in 1931. We have the mortgage and notes here in this Assembly. The Trustee Board of one of our Churches holds a note from us, due Oct. 30, 1931 for $250.00, and Elder H. D. Davis loaned us $137.50 due Oct. 30, 1931, and we promised to pay them in this Assembly Oct. 23, 1931. I think it will be wise for us to repair our building, clear our land and rent it out. I do not think it would be wise for us to sell our school property as some think, because it is a big investment and if we sell we will loose the fruit of our past labor. The land and first building cost about $3000.00; Greenleaf Public School cost $3000.00; furnishing and running, about $10,000 00; interest about $1,500.00; total about $17,800.00. I think we should keep our School Property because we do not know what the future attitude of the State may be toward Negro education in view of the heavy burden of taxation, and we need a school to train our young preachers, teachers, deacons, superintendents and leaders. If we sell we will go from something to nothing and our children will say: "What a foolish thing our fathers did." Respectfully yours,

C. R. D. Whitfield, Supervisor.

REPORT OF FRATERNAL DELEGATES

We met with the Brethren of the East at Uniontown and they treated us fine and made us welcome. It was a great Assembly.

Elds. C. R. D. Whitfield, H. D. Davis and S. L. Lofton, delegates.

ON NEW CHURCHES

Brethren there were no new churches reported.

Elders J. T. Foy,   J. S. Johnson,   W. M. McArthur.
Bros. N. Alston and   W. A. Moseley,   committee.

ON EXAMINATION FOR ORDINATION

Bro. Chief and brothers. We wish to submit our report as follows: Ten came before us and two passed, Bros. J. S. Cannon Jas. Hopson.

We recommend the course of study as adopted by this Assembly for all local preachers. Realizing more each year the importance of trained leadership in the church and the great responsibility that rests upon the entire brotherhood in the discharge of its duties as the instrumentality of moral and spiritural progress, not only in our respective districts but in the world at large, and the increasing demand for efficiency in all phases of our life, makes it mandatory that proper safeguards be thrown around the church. Therefore, this committee has set a certain standard, and those who fail to pass at the Assembly are privileged to appear at the General Union.

We list the following subjects for careful study: English grammar, U.S. history, geography (especially of the United States and the Holy Land), reading, spelling, arithmetic, the Bible and Bible dictionary. We recommend our religious papers for extra reading and the Bible school quarterlies.

Elds C. H. Cordon, J. C. Artice and J. D. Henry, committee.

It was proposed and agreed that Eld. O. S. Lucas be excused from paying dues this session. Eld. Moore of the Cape Fear Conference was introduced to the assembly. Adjournment.

Thursday Night Preaching Service

After many songs and prayer offerings the Chief introduced Elder W. R. Steeley Chief of the N. and W. Assembly, who made his report and brought greetings from his assembly. His address was responded to by Elder C. R. D. Whitfield. The Selma Choir sang a selection and the 12th. chapter of the Acts was read by Elder R. B. Banks, Elder W. B. Parks offered a very fervent prayer. After another song by the choir the finance solicitors took an offering amounting to $5.36 Elder Banks introduced Elder. C H. Cordon of Philadelphia who after singing one of his spirituals, chose for a text: Acts 12:11 "And when Peter came to himself he said 'I know for a surety that the Lord sent his angels and has delivered me from Herod the king and all the expectation of the Jews." Elder Cordon preached a powerful sermon. Elder Banks closed the service. Benediction by the Chief.

Friday Morning Session

The Assembly met pursuant to adjournment, the Chief in the chair. Bro. Louis Britt lined hymn no. 214, Eld. W. J. Hawkins read John 10 chapter. Eld. G. B. Borden offered prayer, Bro. Britt sang 'Bread of heaven.; The Chief pronounced the house in order for business. It was proposed and agreed that the minutes of the previous days session be read, adopted.
Elders Steeley, Hoyel and Vincient bade us farewell. Eld. Parks offered prayer for Elder Gregory who had become ill. Elder W. R. Raynor was introduced and made a helpful talk. Eld. W. H. Peele of the East was introduced and made a few remarks. Adjournment for preaching. Benediction.

PREACHING SERVICE

After a few voluntary hymns Eld. W. H. Moore offered prayer. Elder Fraizer lined hymn no. 250 'On Jordan stormy banks I stand,' and the 90th. Psalm was read by Eld. Graham and prayer was offered by Elder Banks. Mrs. Marie Whitley sang a solo and the obituaries were read by by Eld. W. M. King. Elder Parks introduced Elder Aycock, who chose for a text Heb. 9:27, sub: The Divine appointment, and preached an able sermon, being the funerals of Elds. Ray and Harris. Elder Parks closed with the words of the Psalmist, 'I thought on my way,' and the Holy Spirit permeated building. Collection, $4.01. Benediction by the Chief.

FRIDAY AFTERNOON SESSION

WOMAN'S MISSIONARY CONVENTION

Brothers; We are sending you only $12.00 this year We ask your prayers. The next Convention will meet at Hickory Grove, Kinston, Thursday before the 3rd. Sunday in September, 1932

Mrs. D. S. Parks, President,   Mrs. Mattie Davis, Sec.

It was proposed and agreed that Elder C, R. D. Whitfield remain as Supervisor, adopted. It was proposed that the Council Board be re-elected, Eld. H O. Wiggs being excepted, adopted. It was proposed that Eld. A. Parker fill the vacancy on the Board created by the resignation of Eld. Wiggs, adopted. It was proposed and agreed that the Treasurers remain for 1932, adopted. It was proposed and agreed that we have 3,000 minutes printed in 90 days or, no later than March, 1932. It was proposed that the Assembly settle its indebtness, adopted. It was proposed that the next Assembly go to King's Chapel, Kinston, adopted It was proposed that the Assembly send an official representative to Philadelphia and points north each year. It was proposed by Eld. J. R. Pitt and agreed by Eld. W. W. Webb that Eld. J. F. McLaurin deliver the Address of Thanks tonight, adopted.

After recieving the report of the Committee on Divine Worship the Assembly adjourned until the 7:00 o'clock preaching service.

FRIDAY NIGHT PREACHING SERVICE

After a few voluntary songs the Finance solicitors took an offering, the amonnt being $4.00. (on Thursday night $5.60 for Elder B. J. Gregory) After the regular offering the solicitors raised $8.20 for Sister Elks. Then Elder Aycock introduced Elder J. F. McLaurin who delivered the Address of thanks.

According to the decision of the Committee on Divine Worship that Eld. Faison preach and Eld. Peele alternate, both being present, Eld. W. H. Peele sang a hymn and read the 11 chapter of 2nd. Corinthians Elder Woodard offered prayer. Eld. Peele introduced Eld I. W. Faison who chose for a text Psalms 45:17, "I will make thy name remembered in all generations," Sub: The Memorial name. Elder Faison, in his masterly way held his people spellbound. Elder Peele extended the invitation One was recieved during the session. At the close of the sermon the Chief assisted by Elder Parks and others administered the Lord's Supper. Doxology and benediction.

Thus the 59th. session closed in love

STATISTICAL TABLE,—cont'd.

St. James, Kinston	- - - - -
Mewborn Chapel, Kinston	- - - -
Youngville, Raleigh, C. H. W. Holloway	- -
Zion Light, Norfolk, Va. J. T. Jones	
Myrtle Grove, Sound, G. W. Gregg	
St. John, Scott Hill, G. W. Gregg	
Antioch, Wilmington G. W Gregg	
St. John, Black Creek, J. H. Artist	
St. Thomas, Enfield.	
Heath Chapel, Kinston. J. H. Harper	
Oak Chapel, Selma, J. H. Rouse	

CHURCH, P. O. PASTOR and DELEGATE	Received	Baptized	Excluded	Died	Fin. M. Memb.	Total Membership	General Contributions	Value Church prop'ty	Paid Pastor	Paid other Ministers	Local expenses	Delegate Fee	Preaching Sunday
Alumn Springs, Dover, W. B. Banks	9	9			7	50	2.00	5000.00	75.00	1.75	11.00		1s
Antioch, Clayton, W. G. Best, by letter				30	110	40	5.75	500.00	47.07	18.75	11.00		2n
Antioch, Hookerton, J. C. Artice, Annie Streater	13	13		3	19	29	3.00	1500.00		3.00		3.00	4t
Clifton Chapel, Wilson, P. H. Howell	6	6			2.65		3.15	1000.00	34.79		21.00		4t
Dennis Chapel, Pikeville, K. K. Wiley, Letter								200.00					3r
Eastern Star, Norfolk, J. H. Smith													
Elm Grove, Pikeville, A. Parker	48	32				62	10.00	3500.00	120.00	7.00			2n
Faison, Faison, S. L. Lofton, Letter	19	6		1	30	35	10.00	2000.00	75.00	3.90	28.50		2n
Flat Rock, Sims, R. W. G. Best, letter	11	1			118	118	7.50	2000.00	200.00	7.25	8.00		4t
Grainger Chapel, Grainger, H. D. Davis	7	6		5	175		10.00	350.00					3r
Greenleaf, Goldsboro, C. R. D. Whitfield, Letter	6	2		3			10.00	600.00	106.01	40.00	117.00		1-
Grifton Chapel, Grifton, E. J. Faison, Cora Dunn	55	40		1		160	9.00	1000.00			130.00	3.00	1s
Heather Grove, Greenville, A. Parker						25	10.00	1000.00					1s
Gickory Grove, Kinston. E. F. Johnson, Letter	4	1		2	34	44	16.50	200.00	78.20	19.01	35.80		3r
Holly Hill, Bests, C. R. D. Whitfield. Letter	22	10	1	1		180	25.00	3.00	115.17	30.00	55.00		4t
Holly Grove, Clinton, R. B. Banks, Letter	58	23		3	33	145	12.75	2000.00	80.00		72.00		2n
King Chapel, Kinston, H. D. Davis, Letter	30	19			83	131	7.50	2000.00	81.99	20.00	7.00		4t
Little Creek, Ayden, I. W. Faison, Letter	44	32		2	75	283	14.00	2000.00	100.00	6.00	3.00		1s
Lattis Chapel, A. B. Aycock					18			150.00					3r
Morning Star, Rocky Mt., W. B. Parks, Letter	13	4		4	23	81	8.00	200.00	100.25	15.01	53.01		3r
Mt. Zion, Calypso, G. B. Borden	8			3	80	85	10.00	3000.00	100.00		35.00		1-
Mt. Olive, Lawrenceville, Va. J. H. Smith					25			1500.00				53.10	3r
Pleasant Union, Goldsboro, P. H. Howell, J. Lee	9	4		2		70	4.00	1500.00	61.31		6.00	3.00	3r
Pleasant Grove, Fayetteville, G. B. Borden, letter	9	4				38	7.50	3000.00	175.00		20.20		1s
Pleasant Grove, Freeman, Va W. M. Hopson, letter	5	5				29	4.00	1500.00	10.85	6.50	3.00		2-
Pleasant Grove, Drewryville, Va. Jas. Hopson						20		1000.00					4t
Phillippi, Greenville, H. D. Davis, letter													

Church, P. O., Pastor and Clerk												Sunday
Running Branch, Clinton, J. F. McLaurin	3 11	4		75	3.00	500.00	75.00	10.00	9.00	3.00	3.00	4th
St. Paul, Ayden, S. L. Lofton, by letter	7 5	2 1	25	73	7.00	1500.00	125.00	8.00	9.00			1st
St. Paul, Wilson, S. L. Lofton, by letter	15 4	3	14	154	10.00	1000.00	207.86	13.50	39.00			4th
St. Paul, New Bern, A. Parker, by letter	6 1	3 1	31	35	15.00	2000.00	96.50	8.00	11.50			1st
St. Rose, Wilson, W. A. Fordham, by letter	15 8	3		115	4.80	1500.00	178.57	54.62	120.30			1-2
St. Peter, Kinston, I. W. Faison, by lettnr	33			280	25.00	10000.00	580.00	9.00	498.85			2-4
St. Peter, Smithfield, W. A. Fordham, F. Saunders	14 4	100	100	170	17.00	3400.00	233.00	25.00	25.00	3.00	3.00	2-4
St. Peter, Philadelphia, C. H. Cordon					19.00							Every
St. Peter, Farmville, J R Pitt												
St. Luke, Goldsboro, B. C. Whitfield, J. Brewnton	11 32	6	25	476	2.00	700.00	485.00	75.00	160.00	3.00	3.00	1-3
St. Luke, Mt. Olive, I. w. Faison, Jessie Jackson	26 16	1	75	135	34.10	200.00	150.00		79.05			1st
St. Mark, Stantonburg, J. C. Artice, E. Rowe	12 10	3 2		150	20.00	2000.00	98.75	9.05	7.70	3.00	3.00	2nd
St. Mark, Goldsboro, H D Davis, by letter	3			150	52.00	500.00	600.00	10.00	137.00			4th
St. Mark, La Grange, A. Parker, by letter	16	6 1	28		4.00	5.00	50.00	8.00	12.00			4th
St. James, Fountain, W B Parks by letter	60 25		75	150	8.00	200.00	100.00	25.00	90.00			4th
St. James, Vanceboro, T W R Keys, by letter	7 3		25	88	6.15	1000.00	100.00		16.00			1st
St. James, Elm City, J. R. Pitt	9	0	15	15	4.00	2000.00	23.96	7.56	16.00			4th
St. James, Goldsboro, J H Fraizer	18 5		0	17	1.70	500.00	10.00	3.70	21.50			2-4
St. Stephen, Trenton, E. F. Johnson, by letter					10.00							2nd
St. Stephen, Princeton, A. B Aycock, Wm Masey	4	2	20	20	4.50	1000.00	75.00	8.00	10.00			2
St. James, La Grange, T. S. Simmons					6.00							4th
St. Paul, Clinton, R. Thompson	7		41	41	8.25	1000.00	76.00	21.00	10.00			4th
St. Luke, Tarboro, S L Lofton												
St. John, Dover, J. H. Rouse	12											3rd
St. Matthew, Zebulon, J. H. Rouse												
St. Joseph, Kinston, W. G. Best	25 5	50 4	30	90	7.00	1500.00	168.75	50.00	79.30	3.00	3.00	1-3
St. Mary, Bailey, J. C. Artice ... F. Adams	92 33	1 1	149	249	28.00	400.00	152.55	28.00	91.44			1-3
Selma, Selma, W. A. Fordham, Mrs. W. G. Best	7	1 1	21	67	14.00	40.00	161.86	10.00	275.96	3.00	3.00	1-3
Shiloh, Grifton, J. H. Harper, by letter	17 7		25	43	2.50	550.00	75.00	10.00	6.00			2nd
Snow Hill, Wade, J. C. Artice, Luella Burnett	4 3	8 3		25	5.00	1500.00	67.00	6.20	22.00			1st
Union Grove, Clinton, ‡ F. D. Ashford	20 7	3	50	130	11.00	500.00	60.00	20.00	5.00	3.00	3.00	2nd
Vine Swamp, Kinston, B. C. Whitfeld, John Dunn	61 17	12 5		398	25.00	3500.00	00.10	15.00	5.00	3.00	3.00	2nd
Warren Chapel, Pikeville, J. H. Artice, by letter	9	1	16		3.50	100.00	15.00	1.75	29.75			4th
Weeping Mary, Newbern, H. L. Shepherd					3.61							
Weeping Mary, Arapahoe, James Wilks, by letter		1	7	18	8.00	150.00	124.66	75	6.37			1st
Piney Crove, Araraohe, James Graham			18	31	6.00	500.00	45.00	7.00	4.00			4th
Piney Grove, Woodington, James Graham					3.00							3rd
Zion Spring, Bunn, E. F. Johnson, by letter	15 8	4	45	80	2.50	3000.00	180.00	18.00	43.00			3rd

In Memorium

The Fifty-four Members and
Elders H. A. Whitfield, F. Graham, Alex Berry, J. S. Ray,
J. C. Leathers, Ed. Harris. E. J. Jenkins and B. C. Whitfield.

Servants of the Lord, well done,
Rest from thy honored employ,
The battle fought, the victory won——
Enter thy Master's joy.

Our Dead

Roll of Elders and their Post Office

Elder C. R. D. Whitfield, 216 E. Shine St., Kinston, N. C. $5.00
Elder H. D Davis P. O. Box 16, Kinston, N. C 5.00
Elder S. L. Lofton .... 406 George Ave, Goldsboro, N, C, ...5.00
Elder W. A. Fordham ...R. 2, Box 132, Goldsboro, N.C............. ...... 5.00
Elder J. E, Dunn, R. 5, Kinston, N. C. 5.00
Elder J. F. Whitfield, 1924 12th, St., N. W., Washington, D. C. ....
Elder C H. Cordon, ... 5 00
Elder A Parker, Kinston, N. C. 5.00
Elder W. B. Parks, 901 E. Holly St., Rocky Mt. ....
Elder H O. Wiggs, Wilson Mills ....
Elder B. C. Whitfield, deceased ... . 5.
Elder W. G. Best, P. O. Box 111, Selma, N. C 5.00
Elder J. C. Artice, Faison, N. C. 5,
Elder E. F. Johnson, Dover, N. C......... .... 5.
Elder R. Croom, Grifton - . : . . - - - 5.
Elder L. D. Wiggs, R. 6. Goldsboro, ... 3.
Elder J. L. Lee, Faison, N. C......... .... ' . 5.
Elder I. W. Faison, R. 2, Box 5, Faison, N. C......... ....:..5.
Elder W. M. King, Kinston, N. C. - . 5.
Elder J. R. Pitt, Pikeville, N. C. - - - - 5.
Elder W. M. Hopson, Freeman, Va. - - 5.
Elder R. B. Banks, Macon, St., Kinston, N, C,......... . ... 5.
Elder N. H. Holloway - : - . . .
Elder C. H. W. Holloway, Raleigh, N. C......... - 2.
Elder W. M. McArthur, New Bern, N. C. - . : . - 5.00
Elder J. H. Rouse, Princeton, ... 3 00
Elder J. D. Henry, 104 Stallings St., Clinton, N. C. ... .
Elder J. T. Foy, - : - : - - 5.00
Elder G. B. Borden, Clinton . - . . . 5.00
Elder James Graham, R. 5. Kinston 5.00
Elder A. B Aycock, Pikeville, Route - . . - .
Elder T S. Simmons, La Grange, - . - - . 5.00
Elder James Boykins, Wilson, Box 284 ... . .1.00
Elder J. W. Jones Selma excused .... paid . 50
Elder G. R. Fields, Greenville, N. C. .... — 5.00
Elder J. H. Smith, 2426 Chapel St., Norfolk, Va. 5.00
Elder C. D. Royal, R. 5, Box 24, Clinton 5.00
Elder K. K Wiley, 519 Herman St, Goldsboro, - - - 2.50
Elder W. W. Webb, 511 E. Walnut St. Wilson - - - 5.00
Elder Z. V. Quinerly, Grifton, - - - - 3.00
Elder J. H. Harper. Ayden - - - - 5.00
Elder P. H. Howell, R. 6, Goldsboro, Due $13.00 paid... - - 2.00
Sister F. Pettiford, 124 Dewey St., Goldsboro, - - - 1.00
Elder J. H. Frazier, Goldsboro - - - due $11.00 2.00
Elder J. F. Mc Laurin, 323 B. St., Fayetteville, - - 6.00
Elder A. L. Hart, Zebulon, N. C. - . . - - 5.00
Elder W. I. Hawkins, R. F. D Wilson, N. C. - - - 10.00
Elder J. W. Pitt ....Due ....
Elder J. T. Jones . ...
Elder H. L. Shepherd, Kinston, ...

DUE

Eld. E. Z. Coley
Eld. J. H. Artice(s)
Eld. J. T. Cox
Eld. N. Chapman
Eld. E L. Henderson
Eld. Geo. Barnes.
Eld. W. L. Henderson.

Elder O. S. Lucas, 226 N. Clinton St., East Orange, N. J. ....
Elder H. A. McLaurin, sick ... .
Elder J. S. Johnson .... · ....
Elder W. M. Godwin ....
Elder R. Thompson ....
Elder I. Morris, ...
Elder R. H. Exum ....
Elder J. R. Best ....
Elders James Hill, A. Aulston, S. L.
Kirkman, G. T. Taylor, due each $20.
Elders Moses Battle, J. A. Perry and
J. L. Artice, due each, $30.00.
Elders J. Davis, Jas. Moses due $35.
Elders S. H. Williams, J. T. Barnes
and N. T. Kirkman due each, $40.00.

EXCUSED ELDERS

Elders B. J. Gregory, R. 6, Goldsboro, N. C. ....
    J. E. Wiggs. Selma, N. C. .... _____ ...
    E. M. Cox, Kinston, ' ' ....
    J. Raynor, Kinston, ' ' ' ....

DECEASED ELDERS

Elders H. A. Whitfield, Kinston, N. C.
    F. Graham,   ' ' ' '
    Alex Berry,   ' ' ' '
    J. Ray,   Goldsboro, N.C. ....
    J. C. Leathers, Trenton, N. C.
    Ed. Harris, Spring Hope, N. C.
    E. J. Jenkins ... :.....................

NEW ELDERS: J. A. S. Hopson and J. S. Cannon ....

LOCAL MINISTERS

Brothers Louis Britt, ...$3.00   N. Alston, ...$3.00
        J. L. Dunn .... 3.00   J. H. Hawkins, ... 1.00
        Sam Pearson .... 3.00 ...... Henry Artice.... ....4.00

DELEGATES

Bro. Jessie Jackson ....$3.00.   Sisters Lucille Burnett ....$3.00.
    Frank Adam .... 3.00,   Roana Williams ....3.00.
    E. Strong .... 3.00.   Janie Brewington .... 3. .
    Joseph Lee .... 3.00.   Cora Dunn .... 3.
    John Dunn ....   W. G. Best .... 3.00.
    J. F. Royal .... 3.00.   Flossie Saunders ...... 3.00.
                                                 Estelle Rowe .... 3.00.
                                                 Annie Streater .... 3.00.

DISBURSEMENTS

All of the receipts of this sitting apparently paid out to the 1. Official staff for salaries; 2. Repaying two loans obtained to clear off all claims against School property; 3. Committees, Council service and transportation. 4. Compiling, Printing and distributing minutes. (item no 4, $150.00) Impossible to give detailed report, manuscript was recieved by printer unfinished.

FINANCE COMMITTEE

Brethren. Our report is as follows: Recieved at this sitting, $837.61.

Respectfully submitted, Elds. W A. Eordham, A. Parker, committee.

SUPERANUATE TREASURER

Brethren, I wish to make my report: Nothing recieved at this session. (see 1930 minutes)   Respectfully, J. E. Dunn, Treasurer.

ASSEMBLY TREASURER

Brethren, My report is as follows: Nothing brought over; nothing rec'd.
                    Respectfully, H. O. Wiggs.

EDUCATIONAL TREASURER

Smithfield, N. C, Oct. 24, 1931.

1929..Nothing brought over	
1930 Recieved at Greenleaf Assembly	$473.25
1930 Paid Sister Mary Spencer, superannuate ....$ 5.00	
Short in count.. 20.00	
Total.. 25.00	
Balance...	448.25
Oct. 28, 1930 Paid all on School notes....................	448.25
Bal..	000 00
1931 Due on School notes, principal and interest to Oct. 30, 1931.......	387.50
Borrowed from H. D. Davis and B. C. Whitfield	387.50

And with this we paid and took up all notes against the school property.

Respectfully, C. R. D. Whitfield, Treasurer.

Report of Council Board

The Council Board met pursuant to appointment and transacted the following business. 1. The church at Princeton, we assigned Elder P. R. Mewborn. 2. Rouse Chapel. Eld Fields tendered his resignation and it was accepted and we herewith sign Eld. Henry Woodard to the pastorate of Rouse Chapel. 3. Pleasant Union. At the request of the church we signed Elder P. H. Howell. 4. Running Branch Church. As the pastor Eld. E. Z. Coley resigned indefinitely, we recommend and sign Eld. A. D.

Elds. C. R. D. Whitfield, J. C. Artice, A. Parker, W. G. Best, S. L. Lofton, Chief, J. E. Dunn, W. A. Fordham, Secretary.

Greenville, N. C., Feb. 16, 193?

The Joint Council met pursuant to adjournment at Phillippi Chur
Christ, above mentioned place and date. The devotionals were led b
Asst. Chief Elder Lofton singing hymn 5, "A charge to keep I have.'
Scripture lesson, Matt. 18, read by Eld. C. R. D. Whitfield, pray
Eld. R. B. Banks, second hymn no. 195 was sung, "Not all the blo
beasts." A hand of fellowship was extended to all after which the
Eld. Lofton made some very pointed remarks and announced the ho
order for business. Then there arose a discussion as to whether the
of the Assembly, or the Chief of the Council Board should preside, i
proposed and agreed that the Chief of the Council preside, adopted.
S. L. Lofton and Eld. B. J. Mackey, the Chiefs took up the business i
following order: After a brief lecture by a Rev. King, a visitor of the
the Chiefs proceeded to appoint a Committee on Resolutions as follow:
Elders W. G. Best, W. A. Fordham, A Parker, D. L. Norman,
Moore and Joseph James. Adjournment for dinner.

The devotionals for the Evening Session were conducted by Elder
D. Whitfield singing hymn no. 145, prayer by Eld. B. J. Mackey, s
hymn no. 23 was sung. While waiting for the committee report it
suggested that Elder Whitfield, the Supervisor give a lecture for the
of the connection. He arose and led the way in a beautiful helpful le
which was responded to by Eld. J. R. Spencer, Eld. J. T. Cooper and
W. G. Vincient all of the W. N. District. Elders J. C. Artice, P. H. E
and others made interesting talks. The committee was then rea
report, (see resolutions) and the session adjourned.

RESOLUTIONS

Revised and corrected to Feb. 1, 1932.

1. Resolved, That all money recieved during the sitting of the Ass
shall be reserved for the following pusposes, after all expenses have
paid: One-fourth shall be deposited for the Superannuated and the re
der divided equally for the Assembly and Educational purposes, Golc
and Raleigh District, and Church Extension Washington and Norfolk

2. Each apportionment shall have a different treasurer, and all coll
shall deposit the funds collected in the treasury for which it is collectec
further, that no draft on these funds shall be honored by these treasu
except legally signed by the proper authorities.

Special for the Goldsboro Christian Institute.

(a) Teacher's salary, expense fund and all other expenses shall be
directly by the treasurer of the Education Fund upon requisition b
president of the Institute upon regular forms, signed by the Secretar
Chairman of the Trustee Board, a copy of which shall be sent to the S
of the Assembly and Educational Treasurer for his payment.

(b) The principal shall file a written report to the Chairman of the
tee Board once each month, giving average daily attendance and ru
expense, and report annually to the Assembly, giving complete and c
ed report.

(c) There shall be no transaction of the Trustee Board without the
ledge and sanction of the entire Board. [or]

3. The said moneys shall not be paid out used for any other purpose
out the consent of the General Assembly

4. No minister shall mistreat his wife, or deny being married when
from home, if so any brother may report to the Chief and the Chief
Councilmen for trial.

5. No man belonging to the Disciples shall be allowed to give out
lars, subscription papers or ask aid of any congregation that he is r
charge of for any purpose without permission from the pastor in char

6. No preacher belonging to the Disciples shall be allowed in any o
churches to preach unless he can show printed license from the Ge
Assembly, and no preacher shall be set apart to preach unless he I
common school education, a working knowledge of the bible, good m
and a good Christian character.

7. That all ministers who accept the choice of a church or churches shall serve for the period chosen if possible. and no minister shall promise to, or pastor two churches whose service days and hours are the same.

8. No man coming from the d nominations will be set apart to preach for the Disciples until he understands the Gospel as taught by the Disciples.
No young brother that has been raised up among the Disciples shall be set apart to preach the Gospel until the pastor and congregation are well satisfied that he is qualified, but he shall be given power to exercise his gift by his pastor and congregation, and all local preachers shall co-operate with the pastor.

9. All pastors and congregations shall give letters of dismissal when requested. All members who leave their church for twelve months shall apply before leaving for a certificate of absence. All members that are away from the church shall correspond as often as once in three months.

10. All Elders must be connected with some local congregation. Each Elder is requested to pay to the Assembly $5.00 annually and each delegate $3.

11. Any member of the church found intemperate shall be tried by the church and if found guilty shall be expelled until reformed.

12. That no preacher be found around the congregation of another preacher, if so his license shall be revoked.

13. That when the pastor has resigned a church, or a new pastor called, church shall send a letter of commendation to the Assembly respecting his honor as he has done.

14. That in town a church can be built of new members within one-half mile, and in the country two miles, but can recieve no members from the old church except by letter from said church.

15. I, W. A. James, prosose that no minister belonging with the Disciples who knowingly does not conform to the agreements of the General Assembly or uses his influence in his congregation for the same, shall be elected to any office or appointment of the General Assembly.

16. Any member of any local congregation who does not do his or her duty shall not be allowed any voice in the congregation, nor shall be elected as a delegate to the Assembly, Union Meeting or any other important meeting.

17. That the Assembly request each member to pay $1.00 annually for the Assembly. Each church shall have an Educational Rally Day during the summer and the collections be or go for educational purposes, (Goldsboro and Raleigh) and the proceeds be sent to the Assembly.

18. There shall be a Children's Day service held in each year for the Convention and the proceeds after expenses have been paid shall be turned over to the Assembly.

19. No money or moneys shall be paid out of the Assembly treasury without an order signed by the Chief and Scribe.

20. That all Elders shall attend Union Meetings in their respective districts, failing to do so they shall not pastor our churches, except they have a lawful excuse. Elders that are not pastors failing to attend shall not be appointed to any of our churches as pastors, and the Chief shall be notified and he shall refer him to the Council for trial.

21. That all deacons and officers shall co-operate with their pastor; upon failure they shall be excluded from office. (see 43.)

22. That all ministers who recieve candidates for baptism should baptize them as early as possible.

23. No church shall have the right to elect but one elder to serve during the year, but the pastor in charge has the power to choose any preacher that he desires to assist him on any Sunday during his absence.

24. No preacher coming from the denominations shall hold any charge as pastor until he has been in this Connection twelve months.

25. No Council shall remove a preacher from his church to which he is called or sent except for cause affecting his moral and Christian character.

26. That no deacons have the power to close the doors of the church against the Pastor, or stop him from preaching, but can notify the Chief of the Assembly and he shall refer him to the Council.

27. No church shall run another preacher against the Pastor, but he shall be voted on first. Should the majority of financial members vote against him, the church can vote on other preachers, two or more. This election shall be held in the regular Conference, or on the regular preaching Sunday in September. If held in Conference, however, the members must be notified in advance.

to preach

28. No member shall have the right to invite any Preacher at the church to which he or she belongs except by permission of Pastor or Deacon, and said invited preacher shall not accept said invitation, unless by knowledge of the Pastor.

29. There shall be a Sunday School Assembly held in each Union Meeting District annually, and the proceeds shall be reported to the Assembly.

30. All pastors of churches shall have control of all money raised in preaching service except expense of the church service on said day.

31. No church shall elect a man as deacon who has not been in the church one year.

32. The officers of the Assembly shall be elected annually. The Nominating Committee shall be appointed, one third by the Chief and two thirds by the house, and no one shall serve on that committee who has a difference with the Chief.

33. Resolved, That these resolutions go into effect upon their adoption by the General Assembly and shall not be null and void without the vote of the General Assembly, and all preachers who fail to comply with any one or more of them shall be silenced until he does comply.

34. That all women preachers among the Disciples shall have a pastor and be subject to their pastor in regards to their mission or church

35. Resolved, That the Trustee Board of the Goldsboro and Raleigh District shall not have the power to give a mortgage or note, or borrow any money on the school property without the consent of the Assembly and Chief and Councilmen of the G. R. D. No money shall be paid out of the treasuries of either the Assembly, or the School, or of the Superannuated except by an order signed by the Chief and Secretary of this Assembly.

36. That should a complaint arise against a resident minister, the Chief of the Assembly shall be notified and he shall refer it to the Council if necessary.

37. Eliminated.

38. That no sinner shall be a member of any of our choirs, and no quartet composed of sinners be allowed in any of our churches.

39. That any district assembly organized other than by and under the auspices of this General Assembly in our boundaries shall be considered bogus and unauthorized.

40. That no member or members shall organize anything in any church without the consent of the Deacon Board and Pastor.

41. Be it resolved, That there shall be three special sermons: (1) an Educational sermon; (2) a Temperance sermon, and (3) a Doctrinal sermon, preached at each Assembly, and the preachers appointed to preach them from one Assembly to the other.

42. Resolved, That there be no prohibition against a preacher of the Western District pastoring in the East and Eastern preachers pastoring in the West, providing, however, that the churches represent in their respective districts and each pastor shall be accountable for the collection of said funds and their delivery to the proper district.

43. That all deacons be required to attend Sunday School, Prayer Meeting and other religious service and that on time, else they shall be dropped from office and new appointments made by the pastor and church.

44. Resolved, That we accept the Constitution of the Woman's Missionary Society, except as to salaries, and recommend the following scale: President, $7.00 for the term; Vice-President, $3 00 for the term; Scribe, $7.00 for the term; Assistant Scribe, $3.00 for the term; Banking Committee, $2.00 each per day and railroad fare, or its equivalent.

45. That there shall be created the office of District Supervisor and his duty shall be to sit in the official column and see that the rules of the Assembly are carried out as per resolutions and shall preside at such times as questions involving the Chief are being discussed and he shall recieve ten dollars [$10.00] annually for his service.

46. Resolved, That there shall not be any drums or timbrels allowed as a form of worship in any of the Churches of Christ in our Districts.

47. That all members of the Churches of Christ who are delinquent with with their pastors shall not be allowed to unite to.... any other Church of Christ until such member pays those delinquent funds, and when any pastor resigns a church no delinquent member shall be placed in office nor considered a legal member, neither shall such person or persons be allowed to unite to any Church of Christ Any pastor recieving such person or persons into any church shall be removed as pastor.

48. That there shall be a Ministers' and Laymen's Conference held at the Goldsboro Christian Institute, Goldsboro, N. C., each year in the month of June, for the ministers and laymen of the Goldsboro and Raleigh District and there shall be a similar conference held in the Washington and Norfolk District at such time as they deem appropriate.

49. That the agreement of the Minister's and Deacon's Union relative to the Church Policy be adopted by this Assembly as a permanent guide for the Church.

50. That all ministers be compelled to attend the Minister's and Laymen's Conference in their respective districts, and that ministers be requested to study the questions for discussion in the next session.

51. Resolved, That the Chief shall call the Seven Councilmen together, and preside over the Council Board sitting as a Joint Council.

52. That the Chief and Asst. Chief shall not serve on the Council Board.

53. Resolved, That all Auxiliaries be subject to the Assembly.

54. That all Treasurers who misplace monies entrusted to their care shall be removed from office until the money is replaced.

55. That the Supervisor shall not be a member of the Council Board, by reason of his office.

56. Resolved that the salaries of the Chiefs and Scribes be cut as follows: Chief to be paid $15 00; Assistant, $10 00; Scribe, $15.00; Assistant, $10.00.

57. In case of a vacancy occuring during the intervening of the Assembly by death or any trouble that may occur between church and pastor, the said church shall have a right to elect another preacher, and notify the Chief and Council, and they shall assign said preacher if possible, and any unauthorized minister found interfering in any way with the filling of said vacancy shall be couneiled.

58. That any church desiring to pay its pastor a standard salary shall have the priviledge.

Aim and Plea of the Church

We, the Disci les of Christ of Eastern North Carolina and Virginia, wishing to be in pcomplete accord and agreement on the doctrine of the Church, set forth the following which has been the slogan of the Church for more than one hundred years;

General Aim of the Church: Restoration of the New Testament teaching and practice.

Plea of the Church: No creed but Christ; no book but the Bible; no name but the Divine.

Where the Book speaks, we speak; where the book is silent we are silent. In essentials unity; in non-essentials liberty; in all things Charity.

Annual Report of The Church of Christ

——o——

At.. Name.......................

Recieved .... Baptized ....

Excluded. .... Died ....

Finançial Membership....................... Total Membership.....

Delegate ....

Pastor in charge for 19..........; Elder ....

Elder..was elected in Sept

We held no election, so please send us Elder...........................

General Contribution   .   .   .   .   . $.........................

Next Years Assessment   .   .   .   .   . $.........................

Paid Pastor   .   .   .   . $.........................

Paid Evangelists   .   .   .   .   . $.........................

Paid Local Ministers   .   .   .   .   . $.........................

Church repairs   .   .   .   .   ,   . $.........................

Local Expenses   .   .   .   .   .   . $.........................

For Union Meetings   .   .   .   .   . $.........................

For Sunday School   .   .   .   .   . $.........................

For Education   .   .   .   .   . $.........................

Value Church Property   .   ,   .   . $.........................

Total   . .   .   . $.........................

For year ending...——19........

Filled by...Secretary.

Preaching Sunday...

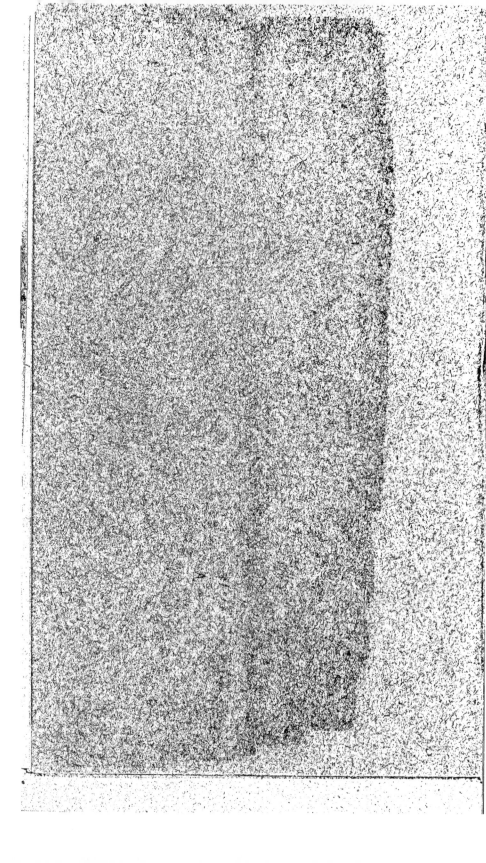

MINUTES

——OF THE——

Fifteenth Annual Session

——OF THE——

Goldsboro and Raleigh Di...

WOMEN'S HOME MISSION CON...

——OF THE——

DISCIPLES OF CHRIST I...

EASTERN NORTH CAR...

——HELD WITH——

HICKORY GROVE CHURCH OF CHRIST...

SEPTEMBER 15-17, 1932...

Next Place of meeting, Morning Star Church of Christ, Rocky Mt., N. C., Thursday before the 1st. Sunday in October, 1933. (Sept. 28.)

Mrs. Daisy S. Parks, President.
Mrs. Laura Levick, Recording Secretary.

C. L. WHITFIELD, PRINTER, 2311 HANSON AVE., NORFOLK, VA.